Sister Nun

SISTER NUN

Shanti Weiland

Negative Capability
PRESS

Sister Nun

© June 2016, Shanti Weiland

Cover and Interior Design by Megan Cary

ISBN: 9780942544411
Library of Congress Control Number: 2016903778

Negative Capability Press
62 Ridgelawn Drive East
Mobile, Alabama 36608

www.negativecapabilitypress.org
facebook.com/negativecapabilitypress

ACKNOWLEDGEMENTS

Many thanks to the following journals that published these poems,
sometimes in slightly altered versions.

"Sleeping with a Woman" *Front Porch Review,* Vol. 6, October 2014

"Coming Out" *the Kerf,* Fall 2012

For my dear friends and colleagues, Michael Bassett and Jordan Sanderson

AND

for Kelley Hudlow. I'm so glad I looked up.

TABLE OF CONTENTS

Nun Assumption #1	3
Every Day, Sister Nun Chops Wood	4
Sister Nun Leaves The Convent	7
Sister in the Arctic	9
Sister Nun Becomes a Cannibal	10
Prom	11
New	12
To Date A Woman	13
The Monster They Made, Part I	14
How Sister Feels in Winter, Part I	15
Nun Assumption #2	19
Coming Out	20
Closet	21
Evolution	22
Sister Nun Faces a Sidewinder	23
Zen Gator	25
Swimming Pool	26
The Monster They Made, Part II	27
The Dissection	28
Werewolf	29
Sister Feeds Them	30
How Sister Feels in Winter, Part II	31
Nun Assumption #3	35
Pageant	36
Sleeping With A Woman	37
Bisexual, Part I	38
Balance	39
Pieces	40
Long Toes	41
Tiki Torches	42

Virginity   43
Rapunzel   44
Marriage   45
Sleep Walkers   46
Temp Job   47
Immortality   48
The Monster They Made, Part III   49
Excerpts From Sister Nun's Self Help Book   50
Sister At Sunset   52
Off to Sea   53

Nun Assumption #4   57
Into the Shell   58
Sister Nun as Universe   59
Go To Hell   60
Where No One Has Gone Before   61
Sister Nun and the Empty   62
Bisexual, Part II   63
Sister Nun As Love Coach   64
Heaven   65
Seasons   66
How Sister Feels in Autumn   67
Sister Nun: Out of Love with Love   68
Bisexual, Part III   69
Gardening   70
She's Back   71
Church of Sister Nun   72

NUN ASSUMPTION #1

Sister Nun tastes
a thunderstorm.
Touch her and
she strikes.

EVERY DAY, SISTER NUN CHOPS WOOD

She didn't care what kind
of nun, and she can't pronounce
Buddhist words. She calls
herself "Sister," splits
a trunk and recalls the day her
mother let the sewing machine needle slip
through her unpolished nail. The crushed
purple flowers slide off Sister's
bald head, poised lightly at her
feet, dense and shattered like her
mother's wound.

Sister keeps his shirt dirty and
secret between the folds of her
robe. A letter falls to her from
a tree:

> *Dear One,*
>
> *You are full of shit.*

Sister grabs her ax.

People get used to strange
things, like two white animals
meeting on a dark road, neither
knowing what the other is.
Sister finds herself like that, early
morning when the pink sun
teases her through the window.
She watches the ceiling warm and
hears the chiming of better
nuns.

She changes her heart to a call
bell, reads about mermaids, with hot
pink cheeks, who slip into the
icy coast.

Sister thinks nothing is more
beautiful than aquamarine
against a red moon. In her
dream, she shifts to snake, humps
up and down the grassy
hill, the sheen of her back, green
on green. A glowing invite.

All is clear after dinner, as
always, before the bells and chanting of
bees stuck to sweet, Sister takes
a forbidden nap and dreams of her
lion half. Licking her mate on the
mane, she awakens to a song:

> *When we hump*
> *I think of horses.*
> *They arrive in separate*
> *colors and sound like*
> *a drum.*

She sneaks to meditation and
in lieu of bliss, finishes the song:

> *Chops the wood like*
> *Snow White's weapon.*
>
> *Plays Marco Polo with*
> *fish, an easy win.*

Sister hates meditation.
His energy feels like a
sunburn. It peels through
the darkness, rattles the bells
and stinks of sandalwood.

The other nuns watch
her slip through the gate.
They know what they
know, and they don't
know what they don't know.

She buys baggies at
Piggly Wiggly, fills them
with water from the slot
machine out front.
Enter fire with a
hose, she tells Water.

The sickness of spring, loud
colors and the aloneness of
breaking from the knowing
of the unknowing, a fuchsia
sun scaring tulips from
the Earth. The tender look
her beloved gave to
someone else.

Like a duck hunter
whose driver is still
in the woods, she vaguely
collects data. His knobby nose
in every single pine cone. She finds
her hand petting a soft lobe above
the collar bone and stiffens her
neck. The empty sun shines
in perfect weather as she rounds off
the last block.

SISTER NUN LEAVES THE CONVENT

Sister stops claiming
anything that won't
claim her back. She longs
to lay an egg.

She leaves the convent but
keeps the name "Sister," as the
divorced do, embarks on a journey
late nights to someone's bed,
hears Ave Maria when she
orgasms, clutches Buddhist
prayer beads.

At the bar, she balances
a ball on her still bald
head, and clicks. Imagines
Karma as a beautiful man,
shaming and rewarding. His hair
a dark, wet branch.

*   *   *

Sister becomes her own
perpetrator, empathizes with
the one who struck her
like a wood cutter.
Kisses a woman with a
masculine grip and ignores
the soft scent of his décolletage.

Sister fears everything
in spring is a trick. The full
breasts she now holds in a
bustier, two airy dandelions,
bright against the rising
storm.

She laughs with fat
Buddha, who releases

vodka when she pulls
his golden hand.

A woman offers her breast
milk. The baby is asleep
under trees, and Sister
remembers her last night in
convent, crawling
the roots, his name tangled
in her phantom hair.

*   *   *

At night, she hears men
calling from the shoreline and
stays centered, floats on drift
wood. Sister likes to be
what she is, and thinks of
her friend at convent and the pearly
peach robe, shimmering against
the water.

Sister dips her
hand into the cold
lake and remembers
that no bee is without
stinger.

She lies on her back and
the night is a sermon: *We are
finished. We must go
back to get ahead.* Sister follows
the line where her hair once
cradled the collar bone.

A frozen embryo,
breathless and alone.

SISTER IN THE ARCTIC

Sister wonders how
many days she can live
alone. She lies
in snow. Licks
flakes. Can't tell
day from night.
She thinks of
her shaved head and
prayer beads
chaffing her
warmth. The space
in summer when his
body felt like
the end.

SISTER NUN BECOMES A CANNIBAL

Like a Kamikaze, she tells herself
it's for love. Keeps the robe from her
time at convent, wraps it as if
going to Grandma's, a glow
in the dark woods. Becomes her own
predator and forgets that hunger
bites.

On the Conga, a python is a
strong arm, loose in the jungle and
needy. Sister leans in, hoping that
bravery lives in flesh, communicable
as ennui.

When she pulls away from the dying
man she's supposed to eat, he throws
his rib at her: *Weak. You could never*
be me!

She stops defending herself and
speaks in blinks, gets why her mother
stopped answering the door when
young Sister Nun, hair shoulder-length and
blonde then, came home from school.

A hot breeze up her skirt, the cars'
exhaust pleading with the city, *Take me*
back, one more time...

Sister rests on a gnarled branch and lets
the muggy jungle perch on the end
of each hair of her buzz cut, shining
in the moonlight until her scalp is a
lacy, gold hood.

When she winks, the mosquitoes lay
flat against the stars, blood bellies, a
fragile mobile, buzzing and alive and
in love.

PROM

Sister remembers her first prom and the
boys who couldn't go together. Each had
sewn matching bowties and had wistfully
ordered a lily.

The school's parents squealed like
piglets in a barnyard until the boys
cried their only defense: ...*lost*
without him...

Sister sees them in town the weekend
of ten-year reunion, the taller one stooped
in his young frame, and the other, stuttering
his list to the deli clerk.

NEW

Reenact the day you
came here, separated
by your own skin. Here,
place your hand on Sister's
back and spin. This is how
it started. Pin the tail or
vomit first until it's no
fun anymore.

Watch the sky's enormous
list of things too dark
to name. Terrorizing
vacuums. A spritz of
color and light; our
ungodly separateness.

The stars look
stupid like that, washed
up and past their prime.
Dark figures at dawn. One
of them is yours.

TO DATE A WOMAN

is a dare. Grab the tail of a
snow leopard who thought
she was invisible. Watch her turn
in anger, wondering
what you're doing here.

Do not be deterred
or too interested. Run
your fingers down the
net you brought, drape it
over your shoulders and pretend
to walk away. Comb your
hair in front of her and
say something smart.

When she borrows your net,
admiring the layers, the dark
missing pieces, gently drag
her home and lay her near
the hearth.

THE MONSTER THEY MADE, PART I

The monster they created became
a friend, eventually, but not until he had
killed everything they begged
him not to.

Like all enemies, they conjured him
from water and intended all
sorts of vague longings be
burned away with a blink.

Sister likes thinking of
him, who never stilled long
enough for a name. The wreath
of blood he laid upon her
scalp, the annihilation of
doubt and distraction. Such
a comfort, the lotus sinking
into mud, for once, the
relief of giving up.

HOW SISTER FEELS IN WINTER, PART I

Blue nights against
  a snow bank.

An icicle tucked
  in the pine.

A deer,
  silenced and quick.

A fever.

A blank slate.

NUN ASSUMPTION #2

Sister Nun teases
a man. Like a dog
that got the bone, it
no longer matters.

Her lips in
bloom, she shakes
like the dead
in springtime.

COMING OUT

First, eggs and flour, and other
expected ingredients
and a chrome bowl and a fancy
mixer or a man's fingers,
until balls of what's to come,
disorderly on the pan.

Next, the thought,
the need to pull the dough
from the oven and check,
nibble its soft edges, its
curves.

Distraction, a salad as colorful
as the tropics in summer. The main
course, a rectangular quiche, reminds
Sister of her old neighborhood, an alley
every other block, exact
in design.

Thinking of things not
real. Dreaming in French
and no memory. The smell
of chocolate in the distance
and finally, a soft bell. The solid
steaming batch, melted
over a cold rack.

CLOSET

Sister arranges hangers and
sock rolls and drafts a
mosaic of boredom. Beige
lips, hot pink eyes, polka-dotted
hair curled toward a wired
smile, so full of contempt
that Sister instantly falls
to the floor in a heap of
hosiery as Snow White
did once with an apple, balled
in her hand and barreling down
the wrong path.

EVOLUTION

Sister Nun dates
an actress, who practices
loving her in the
mirror.

It's a dirty business,
evolving. The legs
of a fish, once grotesque and
condemned, forced
out of the sea through threat and
curiosity. Tiny fish
toes, clinging to
sand. Squinted
eyes and the shine
of lava.

Sister is done
with acting, and dumps
her secrets out of a
bright, red purse.

SISTER NUN FACES A SIDEWINDER

Sister would say that she had lived
a lonely life, if pressed now in
this chain motel parking lot.
Scales as bright as her own
bald head. The cacti, fuzzy and
soft from a distance, wave
at the cars, taking them
for suns.

If she said she was only alone
when she asked to be, that, too,
would be true, but today she faces
a sidewinder, and she stills
like red rock.

*   *   *

Here's a little known fact: Women
were created by accident. As
dinosaurs lay dying, giving up
on their offspring, lightning
struck a stone, and a giant
woman appeared. Her physical sight
was slight at first, and she hopped
around lava and ducked
from Pterodactyls on
gut alone.

She nursed baby Brontos when
their mothers passed. Held their
long necks gently across her
lap. But soon, the comets made them
so sad that they lifted their big, baby
legs into tar pits, and positioned themselves
to the sun.

The woman painted her body with wet
sand and opened her eyes for
the first time as she sank

into the salty Earth, and
waited.

*   *   *

Sister has learned to wait.
And as the snake finally returns to
her cold nest, Sister thinks of the
woman she left this morning, wrapped
in sky, blue sheets, her naked body
heated in the dark room, and with the
look of our first mother, loving and
astonished.

ZEN GATOR

Sister peels off her
winnings and sews a
catsuit of gator flesh.

She climbs the platform, hears
the clank of keys popping off
the collar. He rests his tail
against the ring. Trembling
under the weight, it bounces
slightly and startles him.

Dressed in his image, she takes
a stand. Remembers the gruesome
fairytales of convent. A lioness,
chased by hunters, drops the
baby out of her and
bolts. Alone and still
soft, a herd of sheep raise him on
leaves until the day he meets
himself, and shown his true
place, brutalizes his adopted
family.

Sister hears a mother
bleating as she headlocks this
old lizard, her scalp, peach
against the green.

SWIMMING POOL

It's easy to live when you
think of dying. The heavy
last hand, patting your
back some other way.

As they lift Sister's
body from the pool,
the bold smell of
chlorine, the lights
from the water, all over
her like bells.

But this was a long time
ago, before convent or any
knowledge of life above
ground. Tough back then,
to see black balloons in a
clear, blue sky.

THE MONSTER THEY MADE, PART II

This sort of loss,
the kind you see coming,
feels exactly the same as the
kind you don't. Uprooted
trees shooting through glass.

It's grief that sticks.
The tiny hole that forms, others
find only by accident. Run a finger
along the sill and find a dent.
That dent will always be
a dent and belongs to the larger
pocked mosaic, a mirror of sunlight
and infinite darkness.

Leaving Sister with only one
defense: the innate push
to dodge the bullet.

THE DISSECTION

Sister Nun agreed to it. A small
group of women sharpened knives and
forks and other kitchen tools. They agreed
to agree: first the legs, each one slipped into
separate tubes, no consorting. Her heart, dumped
gently into a tank, crude, with tacky
bath tub stickers. It's how she'd always
seen it. Souvenirs in a basket at a
shop somewhere in Tahiti. Her ears and eyes—
bobbles on a tourist's wrist. Restaurant planters
bloom with her arms: *Hello!* they wave
It's springtime! In this way, Sister has forced
omniscience, twinkling hard against sunset.

WEREWOLF

Sister Nun does not mind that
she's a werewolf. It doesn't
bother her to think of the night
he pierced her back with dirty
claws, infecting her with the
urge.

Dogs bark at the night, prepare
for Sister's visit. She gnaws their
bones, humps the women, and makes
everyone laugh.

But not everybody likes Sister
Wolf. The humans grab their
rifles or, in a pinch, chuck
silver bangles at her and
shriek. Sister growls,
laughs, and wakes nude
and adorned until the next
bald moon pulls her
like a riptide.

SISTER FEEDS THEM

until
they float
with praise
for her
lemon meringue
each to the ceiling.
Balloons, these
people, plum
tarts and filling
the space
Sister reserves
for frescos, remote
spider webs,
chandeliers that
twinkle in their own
world up there.
It matters
to her, how
she whipped
the shadows
of those who
would have her
sugar-free, a
skinny version
of their own
hell.

HOW SISTER FEELS IN WINTER, PART II

The deer gets her
bearings, finally, as the
blood melts sleet beneath
her body. Icicles break
from a dark branch and
reminds her of copper
chimes. Bright dead
leaves cracking under
hoof. Yellow pollen
floating like snow. The
day she came into
this world, wavering
against the rainstorm.

NUN ASSUMPTION #3

Sister Nun laps up
milk like a kitten, plays
herself in a movie about
a woman who is
similarly drawn to
lapping it up.

PAGEANT

Sister enters a
beauty pageant and
spikes her mohawk with
glitter paint. The other
girls rub blush high
on their cheekbones.
Sister paints her face
mime and when asked
of her goals, boxes
them in.

SLEEPING WITH A WOMAN

is a prayer. The first
night of an arranged
marriage. A bright
cloak in the woods,
a silver moon.

A snow globe city,
tiny painted lights. People
inside houses, saying
prayers. The woods line
the bend. A moon against
the glass.

BISEXUAL, PART I

Kind of a disaster, like a
one-woman-band, chasing
down a purse-snatcher.

BALANCE

Falling in love is
reincarnation. Amnesia
to the past atrocities
committed in states that
linger, a vague nightmare
Sister greets like
a virgin at prom. The delicate
ruffle, taffeta bodice, a
curtsey to the lights playing
games with truth.

In fairness, the down
tempo and ridiculous
hope is its own truth.
The pretty sister. The one
that makes illness feel
fair, a necessary speed
bump so that others may
live. The balance of the
dead and the freshly
hatched.

Mourners clutch the
sky, breathe damp morning.
They whisper their hurts to the
evergreens and cuss out
the sun. They are nothing
like prom. Bright deserts.
No camels.

But in the ballroom, the cool
fog remains on bare legs and Sister
sways in the dark. The remarkable
flash of silver.

PIECES

He made them all
puzzles, the little Sister
Nuns with their little outfits
and neuroses, and bright, juicy
things they wanted, Jell-O and
sting rays and firecrackers.
And how sad that the final
piece was never placed because
the Creator died last
minute. His decomposing
body blazes over the
Earth and shines upon
the little Sisters, with their
colorful shoes and bald
heads, every one of them
alight with the love He
gave them, and always and
forever bumping and
falling and lighting the
wick, wondering what's
missing.

LONG TOES

Sister remembers walking on tiptoes to please Mother, whose own toes were tiny buds, sheathed in pink slippers. Sister craned her lean neck toward the counter to see her mother's work, diced green beans and an overripe tomato.

Sister stared at the toes of other moms, some longer than hers and wrapped in macramé clogs. Others uneven, black and white piano keys. At night, the moon casts her glow and Sister watches a spider's gangly, furry legs dust the ceiling and slide down the sheer drapes, managing a shag rug on the way back home.

TIKI TORCHES

They say that no one can
bleach the heart, brighten it
to quartz.

Sister enters the dreams of
her former friends as a
cat, soothes them and cuts their
hair with unkempt claws.
Keeps her lovers'
heads on tiki torches.

Small moons in the garden,
a rose vine at her throat.

VIRGINITY

Virginity is a fragile
canoe. Metaphors are
fragile, too, of course.
Sister knows this but
can't help thinking of
powdered white cleavage
and unattractive doilies.

The absence of color and
all the colors at once. The
lotus, pure and floating on a
muddy pond. But what about
cow tipping, the irresistible
urge to knock down the
innocent? Children dressed
to match the night and in love
with love, snake through the
gold grass and up to that
old girl, mother to a dozen
calves in her lifetime, and
remembers them only
by their markings.

The hush of midnight and silence
of those trying to keep silent.
She brushes her tail against
her own leg, feels the breeze on
her hooves as she drifts from
one pattern to another, brown
with white spots...black and
brown swirls...white and
grey...white and grey.

The half moon takes root and
she dreams of soft
mooing and warm milk.
Silver cars on a distant
highway. The way
things used to be.

RAPUNZEL

Sister Nun wants you
to heal her but can only heal
herself. That's what the books
say. She stacks them by
color, a rainbow spiraling
staircase too uncertain
to climb. The day she lets
her hair grow back, long
enough to reach her at the
top, hoping her beloved will
find the coconut shampoo
alluring enough to risk
the fall. The thorny
brush, the fate that
blinds all reason, crying
to the tree tops, as if they've
never seen this before.

MARRIAGE

Sister plays fashion
games by switching
bodies. Skinny
teens, the stooped and the
middle-aged. Sister never
skimps, organizes her
lives by color and lives
them all at once. Flips
a burger and a pirouette,
lies about the night
shift, winner of the chili
cook off.

Sister learns many times
over to extend the branch
for a quicksand rescue.
But she never does it.
Two people slipping into
Earth is the most beautiful
dance. The silk of the
fall and the sun, darkening
orange, red, blue skies
no where, surrendering to
the staircase of legs, entangled,
dog paddling, and the final
answer to a crass question.

SLEEP WALKERS

In some convents, nuns
sleepwalk every night, tossing
sachets of dead flowers like
maidens at a wedding. In the
morning, they finish their toast
and take bright, blue pills for
their headaches.

Sister's convent slept
hard and didn't take
spirits seriously. Discussed
dreams in the garden and how
to weed the sows from their
pantry.

TEMP JOB

Sister Nun takes a
temp job to find
Zen through repetition.
She sits facing a man's
back and types *Lunch $10*
Lunch $10 on little green
passes while thinking of
nothing, which is
impossible while noticing
the rhythmic ticks of her
cubical-mate, his desk, turned
from the window.

The dominant snap of the
manual typewriter: *Lunch $10*
Lunch $10. His shoulder
blades react
each time as if
for the first. Back from
Vietnam so long
ago, and still utterly,
utterly alert.

IMMORTALITY

When things go
well, Sister wants
to live forever like
a superhero with a
band of immortals
who crawl all over
buildings helping
people out.

When the world is
over, they fire
marshmallows in a
red cave and remember
old loves who
died again and again
throughout the centuries.
Their own beautiful,
permanent youth, changed
a hundred times over,
glittering pink some days,
opaque and withholding on
others. Wings at times,
that which separates them
from the larger pack. Lean
muscle, recognizable to
those who study
immortality or the history
of friendship.

Other times, agony's familiar
noose, a corrective sinner's
flog, Sister longs
to change back to
energy. Watch the
story through the eyes of
everyone else. Blissfully
detached, and a gentle voice,
asking, *Do you like it
here?*

THE MONSTER THEY MADE, PART III

Sister regrets the month she gave up
cheesecake. The lost inch around her waist
was not worth it, nor was believing
the old line "Free candy apples..."

During her seclusion, many suspected
it was Sister who became that
monster, ripped the heads off their
garden gnomes. Planted cynicism and
scratched at it with her plump talons.

Others denied any monster at all:
"A trick of the light," or
a town of "overtired citizens."

But Sister never really
left. Always on the
fringe, and taking everyone
for mirrors.

EXCERPTS FROM SISTER NUN'S SELF HELP BOOK

Like the fairytale man with blades for eyes,
slicing up everything he meant to
love, his sorrowful visions, the blood; better he lives
like a pitiful shadow off in some park with signs
that warn: BEWARE OF MOUNTAIN LIONS.

Compassion, like guilt, is only
useful for a minute before
it eats its own
tail and you
along with it.

These predators are quiet and
sneaky but easily fooled by
height. Mistaking it for
confidence, it may lick its paws
as an act of posturing. A teenager,
afraid to be alone, to be found out
as tender, which leads us right back
to compassion. That crippling tool
everyone uses too much or
not at all.

Too much? Write a really cheerful
suicide note:

Dear Friends and Family,
Don't take it
personally. You all
rocked!

Drown yourself in a
salt water pool; swimming
will lift your spirits.

Talk to your spirits. Tease them
with crumpets they can't
touch.

Romantic seekers in the
woods, heads tilted slightly like a
languid girl's, no longer exist. They are
cramped in city condos. Do not
approach them! Do not eat their
couscous or close your
eyes around them.

And finally, when you see
Buddha, which you often do,
don't tell anyone or they'll
pester you for details. Rather,
let the warmth of his image
surround you like a milk
bath, approach with surrender
and wisdom and a vat
of peace. Then, chop off
that head.

SISTER AT SUNSET

Don't bother
looking. No one
"ends up" anything.

Sunset drowns itself
in pink, only to
creep behind Sister,
again and again, from the
blackest nights.

OFF TO SEA

Sister goes mute
again, hands a large
stone to the latest
man who let her down
the mountain's edge,
gently into still
water, peaceful lily.

NUN ASSUMPTION #4

Sister Nun becomes a spelunker
as all do who love despite the
shame of it. The way the Universe
loves her back, glittery, the smell of
skunk and jasmine, like muggy
nights and the sound of loud
harmonious bugs.

INTO THE SHELL

One morning, the pink sky touched
Sister in a way that reminded her of
convent. The drive to scale the
wall in a grand gesture of escape,
like pantomiming death.

Sister rings her call bell
heart, for old times'
sake, and bathes so long
she scales. Flops
her pearly tail and feels
exotic.

*It's the middle part that's
hard,* she thinks. After the
shock forces you deep
into the twinkling of
your own shell.

She rubs her hands in
sandalwood, tries to conjure
that old wound, agitate it
again to a meaningful
diamond she'll flash at
the night.

To realize the love for
one is just to show up the
other. An endlessly shifting
finish line in an old-fashioned
race. Dim shells on their way
back to the ocean.

SISTER NUN AS UNIVERSE

Casual sex, the half bitten
cupcake. She slips
an electric fence that charges
her heart like an engine.

Sister Nun does not need
you. She's always lived
in twilight, preserved like a
fleeing town, smothered in
lava.

GO TO HELL

On a whim, Sister goes to hell
for the weekend. Originally seeking
her mother, she remembers some old
friends who had moved here years ago.

"Beelzebub!" Five guys turn
around, and Sister thinks what
a popular name that is here. She doesn't
blush, but the lava pinks her all
over. It's always this way, as she assumes
her skeletal form, spreading her wings
like death.

In it but not of it. Pearls of
sweat on the petrified hills and
skinny shadows eyeing her
wishbone.

WHERE NO ONE HAS GONE BEFORE

Sister would like to marry
Captain Jean-Luc Picard of the
Star Ship *Enterprise* and wear
high-suspended collars, brightly
lit like autumn, where all the
shames and dishonors we've endured
or committed, all the garish
wounds, marring the soft skin beneath
our eyes, across our scalps, the
stiffness in our arms, our lower
backs, the stars blinding us with
hope; tamed, refreshed, pressed
good as new within a day, or a
week, as clean and black as a
vacuum in space.

SISTER NUN AND THE EMPTY
For the German maid who ruined Postmodernism

A German maid
cleans the paint right
off *When It Starts*
Dripping From The Ceilings.
Meaning erased, and what
a relief!

There is nothing
that Sister Nun can't take
personally. Like the
mother whose newborn
arrives with claws,
Sister is prone to
blaming art. The coy
painting of a well-dressed
bear hanging ajar above
her bed, influencing
the make up of her
offspring.

BISEXUAL, PART II

Sister remembers when her wings
shined green and magenta against
the winter sun. The strength and
sheer expanse of her flight. Now,
the core shifting, the base of her. Flight
with the bright bones of her skeleton self.
Aerodynamic, sturdy.

When she denies them, these men,
the lovers who found peace buried
in her neck, the trail of their hairy
chests, sweet and unconcerned. When
she pretends the path is elsewhere
only, she dreams of roots that demand
soil, palm trees that graze the sky.
The oppressive hand of a God
she did not create herself.

SISTER NUN AS LOVE COACH

Sister lets romance
"run its course" like the
blade greets a vein.
The strain of reps and
a doomed race, pushing
everything to its best.

A giant palm from deep
in the Earth roots through
soil and abducts Sister,
pulls her to the core.
Fire-forged, her new
heart, the shiniest vehicle
drag racing through space,
winning chicken with every
comet. Shoulder blades scarred
from wings she never got.

HEAVEN

Anyone can get into
heaven if they keep
trying. The cool
blue walls, like the
obvious shot in a
pinball machine.

Sister never stays
long, the praying and
flat notes of the angels
annoy her. Plus, they know
of her abilities, eye her
feet as if they'll
burst into talons.

The disorganized lunch
periods. Grown folk
begging for favors. The
tight comfort of the
mother figure.

But Sister knows that
nobody can be separate
or not alone.

SEASONS

Like any life, on some
days, Sister was a
pearl, pried from a
salty mouth.

Other days, she was a
turquoise bird, fighting
a snake for her first
born.

Sometimes she yelled
at her friends, things
that no one understood:
*You don't know shit
about rainbows!*

Knowing what she
knew, the hell of
cycles. Following
the bread crumbs through
the forest until the
howls sound like
home, where every
flash is the first and
the last.

HOW SISTER FEELS IN AUTUMN

Everyone turns navy
blue, muted and a little
less. Milk in the coconut.
The whippoorwills
strangling each bush.

Sister wears nothing
but blue bells on her
feet, conjuring a silent
hearth beneath her
cool skin, far
from everyone.

SISTER NUN: OUT OF LOVE WITH LOVE

Sister hates trust
games because she's always
the last one through
the furniture fortress, and not
a clue how to file
the experience.

At night, she covers
shallots in oil from a
cherry-colored bottle.
Like a dream, gold
hues, the faint
sizzling just above
the fire. A cat who will
bark at the moon.

BISEXUAL, PART III

The way you watch
your back in winter.
Snow quiets the sirens
Sister used to mock
in summertime as she
sailed by half-clothed.

Dreams are memories.
Satin ribbons wrap
the wound.

Sister misses the python's
muscles, that which can
crush its own kind. She
considers her wolf
nights, waking alone, the
fresh scent of the meadow.

Like a satyr, hiding behind
the buffet table, Sister peers
out at the whole affair, the drinking,
the white noise clearing
her vision. Everyone's the
same. Everyone is
different.

GARDENING

Sister tends all
the parts of herself
in secret, the red
tulips, the sunset
of men she
loved so much.
Crab grass and her
parents at all
ages. Her father,
tall and slim, leaning
down like a slippery
elm, sunshine
attracted to leaves.

Sister weeds nothing.
Not the broken vines or
feminine wiles. Not
sarcasm or her
insufficient hoe.

Sister knows she makes
no sense as her friends stretch
their stems to the stratosphere
without her.

SHE'S BACK

God is *so* glad
Sister's over her
"I'm a lowly human"
phase. Finally
they can pal around
the mall again, write
love songs to pets,
and scorn those
who don't celebrate
their puppies' birthdays.

Fetch on the beach.
God snatches the stick.
Best in show.
Cookies at Christmas,
wimpy devil horns and
pink frosting. Sister loves
snow. God licks the
bowl clean. Hot
times after dark.

CHURCH OF SISTER NUN

In life, Sister always
thought of church as an
unlucky place. The jewel
toned glass, impressing
a false sun. There's incense,
she remembers that, lit
everywhere like perfumed
bugs, sliding down the stick.
Now, centuries after her death,
she's back.

After the span of her Earthly
life, 215 years, she had finally
seen it all. The melodrama
of her broken, old heart.
An impractical paperweight
holding down nothing at all. And
at her age, followers behind her
every step with their future cameras.

Sometime in her 90's she had caught
the eye of a young, male sculptor
(whom she later outlived) and spent
all his mornings creating versions of
her from clay, glass, silk, even trees.
All his lovers were bald. You see,
to hope that someone has reached
the tower and sees you, the village,
and the hills beyond the sea is worth
even more than an original Sister Nun
fetish.

But the truth is, Sister never knew a thing.
And one night, she slipped away
from camp. The boys slept in piles,
clutching the air. The girls, curled
into the Earth, reminded Sister of
something from a long time ago.
Black sky and happy, pulsating
stars as she reached, at last, the
tamal tree, jasmine opening
the night.

ANNUAL SPONSORS

ABOUT SPONSORSHIP

Since 1981 Negative Capability Press has been committed to publishing quality books of exciting and innovative poetry, fiction, and nonfiction. We are a 501(c)(3) tax-exempt nonprofit organization and are designated by the State of Alabama as a Domestic Nonprofit Corporation. Our press is managed by a volunteer collective dedicated to independent publishing. Every dollar we earn is put directly back into our press — whether it is publishing our next book, marketing our authors, maintaining our website or increasing our distribution opportunities. It is you, our valued supporters, that will allow us to continue to publish beautiful, innovative books by amazing authors. We appreciate your support!

ANNUAL SPONSORSHIP LEVELS
Contributing Sponsor - $50–$99 per year
Acknowledged on our website and in our publications.

Supporting Sponsor - $100–$249 per year
Acknowledgment, plus a limited edition broadside.

Sustaining Sponsor - $250–$499 per year
Acknowledgment, limited edition broadside, plus a signed book.

Editor's Circle - $500 and up
Acknowledgment, limited edition broadside, signed book and an invitation to our salon readings.

Donations may be made at www.negativecapabilitypress.org/donate or by sending a check to:
Negative Capability Press, 62 Ridgelawn Dr. E, Mobile, AL 36608

www.ingramcontent.com/pod-product-compliance
Lightning Source LLC
LaVergne TN
LVHW041202080426
835511LV00006B/713